Ravindu

The Sun. The one who shines.

Sonali Deshmukh

BookLeaf Publishing

India | USA | UK

Made with ❤ on the BookLeaf Publishing Platform
www.bookleafpub.in
www.bookleafpub.com

Dedication

This book is dedicated to
my daughters and Ravindu Amendra,
who inspired me to write
poems in English.

Preface

I am an Artist, Life coach, NLP Practitioner
and a Poet at heart.
A Fashion Designer,
and an MBA graduate by choice.
A spiritual person who believes in manifestation
and the law of the universe while having the
heart of a child.

Acknowledgements

To God, for your blessings and loving me.
To my daughter, thank you for
introducing me to Book Leaf Publication.
To my husband for the support and
love and for always being there.
To my neighbours for keeping me cheerful and happy.
Lastly, to all my family and friends for your
encouragement and support.

1. Elegance of Beauty

You are a surpassingly charming baby,
a real means of beauty.
Which appears in your every glimpse of things.
Your sparkling eyes are like twinkling stars,
Full of dreams,
becoming a golden star.
Your silky shiny hair like waves dancing and
dazzling on the shore.
Your enchanting voice,
your sweet and pretty smile,
will promise to take you a hundred miles.
The dimple on your cheeks adds allure to your chubby
cheeks.
You are like a beautiful unforgettable dream that
just came true.

2. School Reminiscence

Heavy hearted sorrow full
Taking the farewell of my school
There drops from the eyes
a solitary tear reflecting feelings
not a show mere.

Going far away from my friends
There remains reminiscence
Bearing change of trends

Day after day
Years after years
There remains
The reminiscence
Of my dears

Reminiscence and Remembrance
Forms the sea
While the waves reflect
a fading me.

3. I Miss you

I think of you in the morning
I think of you in the evening
I think of you in every dream
I think of you every time
I think of you when the sun shines
I think of you when it's raining
I think of you when I'm walking on the grass
I think of you when I feel the gentle touch of dew drops
I think of you when birds begin chirping
I think of you when they sing a song of love
For you and for me
And then when I think of you
The more I miss you
The more and more

4. You make me alive

You make me dream in the day
You keep me awake the whole night
You make me dance on the waves
You make me fly with the wind
You make me happy
You make me delighted
You make me thrilled
You make me Enthusiastic
You make me optimistic
You make me
Dream, fly and dance
Besides all this
You make me laugh
And your laughter
Makes me alive

5. Return it

The dreams that wear decorated
Return them to the eyes.
The heart beats that wear taken
Return them to the heart.
The nights that wear stolen
Return them to the dreams.
The promises that wear asked
Return them to the past.
The songs that wear sung
Return them to the melody
The tears that wear cried
Return them to the eyelashes.
The shades of gold that wear taken
Return them to the sunset.
The shore that was invaded
Return it to the ocean.
The support that was taken
Return it to the arms.
Just the moments spent with you
Return those back to me.

6. My Dream

One night God appeared in my dreams.
Through the dreams
He entered my heart and took me afar.
We travelled for hours
to reach the garden of flowers.
The flowers there smelt so good,
made me happy and bloomed my mood.
Birds were smiling and cuckoos were singing.
It made me smile and my mind went humming.
It felt like I was flying higher and higher
So light that I could touch the sky.
This is the one dream I always want to have.
If you ask me the reason, I don't know why.
All I know is that I could hear
the pounding of my heart.
Flying high and sitting in the cart.
Oh God, hold my hand
And never let me land.
Oh God, hold me tight in your arms.
And keep me alive in your heart.

7. Seven not just the number

Those beautiful seven colours we see in the sky.
Those horses who pull the cart of the sun.
Those seven days that keep us going
Through the cycle of the weeks.
Melodious music comes out of this.
Those monuments we call the wonders of the world.
How can we forget those sisters that flow?
Among these are the continents that tie them all.
Last but not the least, let's not forget
Success, power, wisdom, and wealth
Fame, energy, and health.
These are aspects of life
That give us motivation and life.

8. In search of peace

In the search of peace
I set out to travel on a unique path
With all my beliefs,
All my faith within
Carrying all my strength along with me
In search of a beautiful treasure.
Breaking the boundaries of realities
And in search of peace.
I found spiritual worship within me.
Finding my own existence within me
With deep faith, creating my own peaceful space.
I travelled back with this precious treasure
Back again to this real world
for a new peaceful spiritual journey.

9. Oh, my little angel

Oh, dear my little angel
You entered my life and made me smile
The moment I heard your voice
It felt like I was in a different universe
The moment I saw you
I jumped with joy and happiness.
You gave meaning to my life.
You give me a reason to live.
Life is fair to me.
I got the gift that I dreamt of.
It gave me the strength to live.
You give me a reason to shine.
I wish you all the happiness.
I wish for your well-being and all the joys of life.

10. Do you know

Oh, universe do you know
Why am I so happy today?
Oh beetles of the night,
Why is my heart singing?
In this season of spring,
Why am I dancing?
Oh, those passing clouds,
Why is my mind running away from me?
Those lovely flowers,
Where does their fragrance come from?
Oh, those valleys, hills and mountains,
Why do I feel like running around you?
Oh, dear butterflies
Why is this world so colorful?
Dear water fountain, do you know
Why am I singing?
Please tell me my soul
Now who is singing my song?

11. Sea shore

I love the seashore
Just like i love sky, birds and flowers
When I get time in spare
I go and walk on the shore.
I call the sand near me
and build the castle which i dream.
Those waves that rises rapidly
I feel like waves of emotions
Swept over me.
I wonder when I look at those
Waves with the rising and falling
Motions,
rise and fall and again rising
Just like the sun who is just setting,
It seems they are giving
A Message for life and living.

12. In search of

A traveller in search of the destination.
A wanderer who is always in search of knowledge.
The wanderers in search of shelter to stay the whole
night.
Those lonely valleys are in search of the travellers.
Just like the mountains
In search of the climbers and trekkers.
Even the darkest night
Is in search of light to illuminate.
Just like everyone is in search
Of awakening and enlightenment.

13. Come Again

Once in a while
Come again
Let the flowers
Bloom again
Let the peacock
Dance again
Let the rain
Shower again
Let the birds
Fly in joy again
Let the rainbow
be formed again
Let the song begin
Let us sing again
Once in a while
Let the spring come again.

14. What if?

What if I am not a poet?
Still, poems flow in me.
What if I am not a Bird?
Still, l want to fly.
What if I am not a storyteller?
Still, I can tell a story of life.
What if I am not a painter?
Still, I can paint the town red.
What if I am not a sailor
Still, I can cross the ocean of
emotions.
What if I am not an achiever?
Still, I can be a dreamer.
What if everything not come
true?
Still, l I am a believer,
What if I am not alive?
Still, I can live in your heart.

15. Concern

I am not concerned about the sunset,
I only care about the sunrays.
I am not concerned about falling,
I only care about rising up.
I am not concerned about the darkness,
I only care about the bright light.
I am not concerned about the emotions,
I only care the space they take.
I am not concerned about rains,
I only care about the floods.
I am not concerned about the drops,
I only care when they flow through my eyes
I am not concerned about anything
I only care about the life,
that taught me to rise and live.

16. Memories are alive

There is sunshine now
But still a little darkness remains.
The dawn is still there with
the accompanying fog.
The days have passed but still
It feels like the beautiful evening
Is yet to come.
All words are spoken but
Some phrases are still unsaid.
All the dreams are shattered
But still the hopes are alive.
All moments are passed
Still the stories are unfinished.
Every wound is healed
But scars are still there.
Everything falls apart
But the memories
Are still alive.

17. Journey

The journey of life is about to begin
when the eyes are wide open.
It feels everything is fair
till the day unfolds layers by layers.
It's a journey without raffles
Still life gives you blind vouchers.
This is an unfulfilled long trip.
Just jump and dive on it.
You have to still go further and further
Against the Strom and war.
It feels like getting closer to
the final destination but......
when you turn around to see
how much you have travel,
It feels like again, the journey
has just begun.

18. My soul

My soul travels with me
In the past and the present.
It travels places I travel
When I was a child, teen and adult.
It goes through ups and downs
the moments I lived in sadness and fear.
It travels through the winds
the rains and the clouds.
It travels through the silence,
the thunder and the clouds
It experiences the happy, sad and
every moment I suffer.
It has gone through every stage of my life.
Whether I am asleep or awake
It has lived every path of my life
it lived every moment
whether I am dancing or singing.
It lived every path of my life.
And now I am not there but...
Still my soul sings the song of my life.

19. I created my universe

I created my own universe
I am the queen of life I own
I have my own universe
Living the life on my own terms
If you want to visit here
To find the beauty of life,
Come through your mind
But through the eyes of mine.
Lots of effort has gone in
To create this world
When you enter here
You should be humble
And down to earth.
With lots of positivity and lots of love,
You have to stay there.
Just like a child, you once were.
This is the universe I created on my own.
I am the queen of the life I own.

20. Thanksgiving

On this occasion of Thanksgiving
I thank you for this opportunity.
Thank you for keeping my heart out there.
To explore the world of poetry
And experiment with words.
A part of my heart
Beats twice the way it used to.
And that is when I realized
How my poetry is almost finished.
I realized it is like
A little princess has grown into a beautiful bride.
A little shy and a little lost, but full of self-pride.
And now I am ready to share my feelings
With the world out there
Through my views and through my dreams.
These stories are all out there.
It feels like they were mine, and now yours.
Have a look and take a feel.
Come and explore
and find out more!

21. Gratitude

I want to express gratitude to the almighty.
For guiding me and giving me light.
Gratitude to the universe
and all the living beings here.
Gratitude to my future ahead
and the best journey I have had
Gratitude to my aura
and to my life.
Gratitude to my soul
and the soul in you.
Gratitude to the Book leaf publication
for bringing out my poetic side.
And finally last
but not the least
I want to express my gratitude
to my present and my past
till I breathe my last.